Dinner In

Attrac

First published 2020 by Fly on the Wall Press

Published in the UK by
Fly on the Wall Press
56 High Lea Rd
New Mills
Derbyshire
SK22 3DP

www.flyonthewallpoetry.co.uk

ISBN: 978-1-913211-06-6

Typesetting and Cover Design by Isabelle Kenyon.
Cover Image by Attracta Fahy.

A CIP Catalogue record for this book is available from the British Library.

LOTTERY FUNDED

Supported using public funding by
ARTS COUNCIL
ENGLAND

On Dinner in the Fields:

In absorbing a new collection of poems, the nature and sensibility of the poet sometimes shines through like unexpected sunshine. Attracta Fahy is seer and chronicler, not of history as we've been taught it, but of a past speckled with folk memory; she is a seer into hearts, into the sensuous rush that sometimes defines what being human means. The world of nature—with foxes, swans, and emblematic creatures—moves her as much as the world of injustice, in which women can be diminished by home and society. This is sensitive, reflective work, rooted in a vision that is both beautiful and existential.

Mary O'Donnell, Maynooth

It is with great pleasure that I endorse the poetry of Attracta Fahy. Hers is the true poetry of the soul. From the depths of her intuitive self her poems speak to us of the archetypes of the collective unconscious. Whether we read them in solitude or hear them spoken they give us a sense of our connectedness to the universe, to nature, and to each other.

Máirín Ní Nualláin, Psychiatrist and Analytical Psychologist

Attracta Fahy's poetry is loaded with explosive material and hits the reader like a tornado. Her poems are rich with perfectly chosen images which couldn't but move the reader. Indeed, if these emotionally raw poems don't make you sit up and listen you should perhaps go to THE doctor to check if you're still alive.

Kevin Higgins

Appearing in journals for some time, Attracta Fahy's poems now find their home in Dinner in the Fields. Like the ancients, she bears an attraction for the depths and modes of spirit, our humanity among the deceased, in lyrics of moving recollection. Here we find the strict codes of rural life, turf fires, gravestone etchings, the character of fields, maw of slurry pits, the waves of migratory birds whose rhythms map our own instincts of homing and displacement.
None of this dissolves in the treacle of nostalgia. Indeed,

throughout she turns to address perils of our collective present: the sham of orthodoxy, the threats to intimacy, the border dividing possession and belonging, and the psyche's slender dominion. But in the grip of these complex and often conflicting subjects, her premises join hands with her intimations: the hope that love is never far, that death cannot cancel meaning, which is always at hand, that family is continuous with history's etchings, that the self grows concurrently in nature and family. As she writes, "hope/ moves in the soil beneath/ my feet." If soil does anything of the sort, we are lucky indeed, and fortunate to have a poet of Fahy's evocative talent to offer the beauty of it to mind. Further, it's work that should be taken to memory.

David Rigsbee

Attracta was the invited poet to this year's Bard Summer School on Clare Island. This year's reading was a huge success.
Attracta has a very autobiographical style to her poetry. She took us first into her childhood and the two graveyards she lived between. Her poems picked up the everyday stuff and everyday rituals that were all around her. Somehow this "stuff" was always rich in meaning. Somehow also the rather morbid setting belied the feelings we were left with as the poems shared the formative symbols and doings of a young life. And like a good Celt, the dark preceded the light!
Moving on, her subsequent poems became an unusual mix of the very normal and the very abnormal. The simple 'playing house' mixed with extraordinary insight into the world of an anorexia patient. Whether normal or abnormal, the poems offered rich material on which to reflect. The work offered some guidance without ever drifting into a didactic space.
As a listener, I am left with a number of abiding images. There was a delicate gentleness in the tone and the content of the reading. Yet this is one strong lady and one strong poet with a strength carved from the journey.

Sandy Dunlop, Director - Bard Mythologies

For my Children,

Deocain Emmet, Caolán, Áille.

Acknowledgements

Acknowledgements are due to the editors of the following publications in which some poems or variations from this collection were first published:

Orbis, Banshee, The Curlew, Poethead, Impspired, The Lake, Crossways, Boyne Berries, Bangor Literary Journal,
The Commorant, Coast to Coast to Coast, The Blue Nib,
Dodging The Rain, Cold Coffee Stand, Ink, Sweat and Tears.

The Tuam Mother and Baby Home – shortlisted for the 2018 Over The Edge New Writers of the Year.
Woman in Waterside House – long listed in North West Words 2016 poetry competition. Included in Anthology 'Her Other Language,' Of Mouth - Northern Women's Writing 2020.

Gratitude is due to Mary O'Donnell, Kevin Higgins and David Rigsbee who have followed and supported my work through discussions and helpful edits.

Sincere thanks to those who read and gave feedback on many of these poems, particularly the participants of the Over The Edge workshops.

Huge gratitude to the poets whose poetry and wisdom has encouraged, inspired, and guided my path throughout life.

Deep love to my children who are a continuous well of inspiration, family and friends, particularly the women who have had my back as I walked this journey.

Contents:

The Woman in Waterside House   8

HyBrasil   9

Etchings   10

Red   11

Moonworld   13

Enduring Utopia   14

Vigil   16

Who I Could Have Been   18

Dinner in the Fields   19

Wintering Swans   20

The Priest Said   22

Sensual Nature   24

It is 3am   25

Picking Potatoes   27

Each Others Opposite   28

When One Lives On Memories   29

How Did I Love You   31

A Diagnosis / My Daughter Speaks   32

Nesting   33

Our Sleeping Women   35

Fall On Me   36

The Tuam Mother and Baby Home   38

Waiting   40

If I Tell the Truth   42

Perhaps   43

The Woman in Waterside House

I have no reason to trust sympathy,
when I tell you I hid for thirteen
days, waiting for marks to disappear.
I'm asked if I provoked him:
the guards call the beating,
'a domestic',

social workers, and welfare,
insist boxes be ticked.
Slight disgust in their faces.
'Even so, when you're leaving,
look for maintenance'
and then the forms, and forms,
and the council informs me
the waiting list is years long.

And the judge doesn't want to know,
"Perpetrators", he says, "have rights."
He convinced me
that I cannot live without him,
I am nothing and no one cares.

I'm alone.
I cannot leave.
Easier to pretend my life
is full, than to face the shame
in your eyes, mine,
and the shame of the world,
when you are a woman with a fist over your face.

Hy Brasil

Out of nowhere you appear in fog,
every seven years vague outlines
tease the faint horizon,
visible for one day, then
you vanish back to myth.

I'm moored, enchanted, longing
for this fabled island erased
from nautical charts.
Here on the mainland we are
unforgiving, overindulged, ignoring
the beauty.

I'm anchored, in love, tied like a boat
to your image.

It's said a wise old man lives in you,
holds gold, silver, jade.
In a stone castle, a magician moves
objects by sound, musical airs in wind;
we cannot hear them from here,
machines, arguing block our ears.
It's rumoured monks with ancient knowledge,
hide in caves, crevices, woodlands,
live on mussel, crab, winkles floating
in pools, elderberry, dandelion, nasturtium.

It's even claimed you've advanced civilisation
across our globe. Here, we have
moved backwards.

Etchings (IHS).

There will be no miracles in a graveyard
amongst the dead, little happens
in the quiet presence
of departed souls.

Our 17th century graveyard
cradled our house: became my home.
Tall slabs like brothers, guarded tombs.
Tiny wildflowers, buttercups, in old grass,
a welcome colour to the dead.

At least spirits listened.
Tension cannot hear,
it cannot bear even its own silence.
Spirits heard, without ever a word.

Fumbled walls of stone reveal their bones,
holding slabs with words in ancient tongue.
The intricate letters, hidden names,
once carved with grace, now corroded
beneath its lichen.

Slipping little fingers through each line,
clearing moss, powdered lime.
A child traced slowly into life,
Etchings.

IHS. (Old Greek version of Iesous, (Jesus) which the Romans adopted
and then used the abbreviation of IHS. This is carved on every 17th
Century Gravestone.

Red

After her father's death she needed
a new bag, a red one, 'a particular red',
She searched, described the colour:
not the brown red jasper, carnelian
or sardonyx, stoic like stale blood,
the fire-red of scarlet, zircon,
flaming fluorite flames of hell.

Not caring for dark rose, blood red rose,
rosewood or even a rose itself,
she continued her pursuit, not magenta,
garnet, or even red topaz —
too dark, they felt murky, dim,
even vermilion looked dainty.
Everyone tried — salespeople,

traders, desperate to sell,
appease and please, 'No' she said,
'No'. She needed this bag,
this exact bag, the colour specific
in her mind.
Not jasper, fire opal or sard — although
patterns are appealing — not opaque,

chalcedony stones of the high priestess'
breastplate. Merlot felt obscure, shadowy,
and too rich. She bought red shoes,
tourmaline, not quelling her longing;
this bag, colour, stone, haunted
her travels, she needed to find it.
Crimson could suffice, virtually

there, this hunt could leave her bereft.
She explained that the red orange of
carnelian felt weak, it would not carry
her identity —a woman now — and the pink
red agate, amaranth and coral seemed
too youthful. Still in her prime,
the extremely rare beryl appeared

exceedingly old, barn red burgundy
like lava, too strong. Salmon although
elegant, robust, was fragile and flaky
when cooked, orange red amber
could calm. Tired in search of her red,
unable to unearth that colour, the search
for red defied her. She gave up.

Her friend called. Just back from holiday,
she had found the perfect bag - Imperial Red.
Within, her gift, an antique ring, gold,
with a red stone: fire ruby.

Moon World

"It's lonely here," I said,
to my son, my ears
holding his voice, travelling
thousands of miles through ether.
My eyes gaze
from the window, moon floats
on night sky, stars watch.
"I miss you,
maybe I could visit."

"Mum, you cannot follow
your children around the world
looking for meaning, Go by yourself,
or stay at home and write a poem."
Through the lump
in my throat I muttered, "True."

Enduring Utopia

They, the soul eaters, sons,
daughters betrothed to institutions,
have usurped my womb,
my sun, ravaged my mind
with privation –

now they want my body.
I am slave, at the mercy
of food, a weapon, it chokes

me with their need.
They think I am frail, bring plates
with teeth, wild animals attack me.

I cannot tell you, as you come
towards me with your large
platter of nourishment, I am

terrified it will eat me,
that blood in its contents
will soak my bones, trigger

primitive instinct. My stomach
refuses to digest your utopia,
where the witch's flame is quenched.

My gut has a voice too,
she becomes a wild animal, bloated
with feeling, fat with lies, seeks

revenge for the killing.
She eats not just your food, your
plate, your power, she swallows my smile.

I've built a wall of starvation.
No one enters, not even me.

Vigil

I walk
to my parish,
over the five fairy forts,
climb church stiles
that once led believers to Mass.
Four paths, through fields
to the 17th century church,
hidden amongst overgrowth,
bramble, briar, whitethorn, and clump.
Only faint outlines of stone, hidden in ruin:
time's watermark.

Speaking in silence, walls tell
our history, famine, eviction,
emigration. TB.
This parochial fold lived dutifully
despite hard times. Entombed
in sacred grass, they will us to learn
their lost history, complete the work,
theirs and ours.

I imagine turf fires, safety from the cold
of fear and pillage,
recall stories
of survival and defence.
I walk through what was once barren,
now fertile fields,
call, invoke the names: Chapel field,
Back field, Race field.

Then on, to the road my forefathers
trod to the old school –
the only heat, sods carried each day.
Past the red pump,
once important, decorative now.
I see the clods and marks of cottages
that once housed people I knew.
They have left, the storytellers, all dead.
I call out again to the people
I knew: Raferty, Flanagan
O'Keefe, Hussey, Whynne, Melody...

Who I Could Have Been

It was never the sheltering trees that started
the fight, stretching their long legs
deep into soil, arms breaking through hard ground,
bending around stone.

It was never the flowing streams
returning to source, wild sea, hiding its beast,
nor the innocent birds flying mid-air, fleeing
without faith, that started the conflict.

Who did this? Took me from her that sat
on the windowsill at night, singing to stars, sky
stretching itself out over the startled moon, sailing
its mouth an O of amazement.

Because I have chosen another does
not mean I've betrayed the child who loved crows,
dark cloaked wisdom women, a raven that flew
from the left shoulder of Chú Chulainn.

I'm still here, dreaming of the life
that could have been, I am still her,
the child who could have saved the world,
or not have done anything except survive.

Dinner in the Fields

I remember you
arriving to the fields
when we saved the hay,
bringing the sweet taste
of dinners, encased in Tupperware,
sitting, sheltered under haycocks,
in the warm sun.
We rested our young bodies
from sweating our work,
tasted the bright tang of cut grass,
drinking sugared tea
from Miwadi bottles,
our dinner in the fields.

After,
we waited again
for you to come
in the evening.
Buttermilk our snack
between your arrivals.
Longing for tea,
we quenched our dusty mouths.
Finally, the sunset took us home,
before another long day,
bodies stretched in the light,
making hay.

Wintering Swans

Three swans
      over my house,
            In vee formation they head north east of
                  veer towards the Mayo mountains,
                       an incredible feat. I hear
                           when dragged
                              my left,

tiny
    craniums compel
        bodies to follow.
                The courage it takes, enduring pain,
                    preparation before flight. Families
                        know when it's time to
                           to seek heat, food
                              wings fly
                                    ice

Across
    the sky, black rims coast,
                long dandelion beaks, trumpet the advent of a wintering
                    Loud vowel conversation honks, susurration
                        reverberate, drone babble soars to
                          A robin, disguised as leaf,
                              across the path.
                                the

where you're planted.'
What then of migratory swans,
their habitual nature, no image of god,
though they find their way.

Lough Corrib,
blue haze beacon,
sounds, like the bins rumble
on gravel, lids flapping. On
large and exquisite birds glide
              over trees, white feathers float,
                        flap mid-air, long
                                  necks stretch
                                            into their
                                                      future,

intuitive
in transit
leave a cold land, arctic islands,
for their young. Strong
over polar sea, skim predators,
caps, storms, white bodies
              sail over obstacles,
                        whoopers
                                  arrive in
                                            Samháin

home.
sound in circles,
mist grey sky.
tumbles in gust
I look to
children of Lir, reborn, fade
              into cloud horizon,
                        Zen Masters say,
                                  'Grow

The Priest Said

There was nothing dignified
about my father's death.
He drowned in a slurry pit.
It was a cold wet Saturday
evening in March – people
going to Mass,
followed the priest,
to our shed, in the field.

I had slipped amongst them,
unnoticed, searching in hope
of finding him alive, while hearing
their prayers for his dead soul.
I watched from a distance,
the ambulance, fire brigade,
guards, and neighbours with slurry
tanks, to empty the pit.

Shrinking into gut-wrenching
pain as the search had continued
for seven hours.
I was there when he was pulled
out, like a calf just born.
Later, sealed in a brown bag,
he was thrown inside our front door.

When he called to our home,
the day my father was buried,
the priest remarked
what a dignified family
that people had mentioned,

we were; we had not cried.
My siblings proud of his praise,
I stayed silent.

Sensual Nature

What if Eros
was also a tender leaf
falling in autumn,
or a marigold,
striking light,
decomposing in soil?
The wind gathers, travels
into every crevice,
as the months move.

I sit in sunset,
watch swans float
on Lough Corrib,
how they arrive
at the brink,
and observe.
Seagulls speak to me
from other worlds.

When the stars dance
they arrive at night
in a sheet of sparkling
pleasure, into our hearts.
My heart also moves,
raw and bright.

It is 3am

We slip into morning, walking Merchants Road,
our feet pace the moon, its timeless light, cloaks,
just enough to dull this truth: I was young once,
no need for fragile kiss, eyes that search
for depth. I want them back,
those days my body flowed, dared adventure, like
trout dancing water, when boys were eager, young starlings
splitting air, and I would tease.

One street away, we could take a night boat, sail to Mizen
Head, sit on peninsula, between rocks, coral, collect shells.
Although I don't know you, we have a relationship.
I would go anywhere tonight.

Still here, I slow to the beat of your steps, tall grey buildings
shadow our frames. We smile to each other, glance
at empty cars, parked like soldiers into little squares.
I've moved in circles, tasting paths to love, never
found the one,
now there's you.

Omnivores, we crawl, afraid to arrive at each other.
Whispers gather, fall around your feet.
"I don't want anything to change," you say.
'It won't," I answer, turn to look away, smell lilac from
my garden mist, standing on concrete path.
You reach your hand to mine, our fingers soft,

I cannot hold this moment.
I'm falling again, wrapping myself around your coat, ink hair
sweeps my face, my chest taut,
feels your dragon breath on my skin.
I'd forgotten what it is to have my body touched.
Our eyes reach, too deep to look, turn again,
under the streetlamp, my mask slips, no words hold
its scaffold, your silence mutes my metallic tongue.

As we arrive, I conceal panic, like water hides
a swan's underbelly, its feet a wheel of passion. Night
echoes,
"I must have the dream of love, your touch,
rush to feel again, embrace what you will offer.
I want to gather stars, wrap us in their shawl,
I'm in the mood, too soon I'll be forgotten."

Picking Potatoes

We walk home from the fields,
our young backs arched, aching,
from spreading slits.
Row after row
we lean over these same furrows,
in autumn,
picking ripe potatoes.

Tired bodies pacing home
in evening sun,
crimson growing beyond our hill,
little said, unable to say
the unspeakable, mindful,
waiting for rest.
Rolling limestone walls,
insular, hold a fantasy,
a world outside
our carpet of green fields.

Security too
in the disipline of work.
With tasks well done,
we believe in a greater life.
Longing connects us to fields
beyond our world.
We will grow into what we leave.
Almost home, our tea is waiting.

Each Other's Opposite

It's December. Through my glass
door I see a rare foxglove
bloom. In erratic times,
pink tubular bells dance
in the shadow of death,
the last fallen leaves.
Trees, naked, stretch long
Kali arms, hands into a dull sky,
live a surrendered life.
In the grey between
dawn and dusk, I watch nature,
how she nurtures her family.
You are everywhere, a stranger
in my house, we are silent,
each other's ghost opposites.
It is snowing and three robins,
centre near the garden
table share one feeder,
without conflict, I call it Jerusalem.
Inside, the heat turned up, a wasp
moves from under the radiator,
attempts to crawl a slow, measured
expiration across the wall. I want
to help, know, it's not the time, life
finds its way. Outside, cold turns
ice, a distant bird soars into the harsh
north sun, too high, disappears.
I gaze at the mirror, holder of shadow,
many faces. We dreamed ourselves
into these images, the opposite of being.
I am ready again for the world,
as I think of the surly waiter who smiled,
full with contraries.

When One Lives On Memories

This is not how I'd planned it,
sitting alone, late afternoon,
nodding at thoughts,
the piano waiting, sunbeams
on walls, the comfort of blue,
starlings ruminate,
build on my roof.
Violets, tender with light,
cover the windowpane,
sunlight pours over walls,
while photographs hold still
moments captured, the mirror
blotched in sapphire
shadow, clouds ghosts.
I have time never imagined,
no more youth, it has passed,
held now in the pause between
tick, and tock.
I hear crows —
it will rain.
On the street there is noise
cars scramble, voices
rush to be heard, pass
into distance.
Powder blue sky
steals over the rug, the mauve vase,
a rose lifts life to this hearth,
its beauty lulls thorns,
scent steals stale from the air.
No, this is not what I'd planned.

My shawl thrown over an ancient chair,
warmth without fire, the squares of my home,
the lines, and circles hold me to the world.
But there are cats crying somewhere
in hidden alleys.

How Did I Love You

On my knees cutting the grass verge
of your path with scissors,
digging weeds from your soil,
creating a perfect ground for your feet.
I loved you as far as the longest straight line,
and back,
the cataclysmic spread of galaxies,
crashing stars, that after millions of years, still
flicker light on a raven night, atoms
falling, gold to my heart.
I loved you like galvanised waves spread
in rows over terraced homes, into horizons,
the unison of a thousand starlings preparing
for flight.
I loved you in sounds, creating a dance
in your honour.
I loved you like a bucket loves to carry,
this vessel leaking water, her life,
loved like warm dandelions cover fields,
dying when pulled, you were my soil.
I loved, walking barefoot, my feet
took me over bramble, stone,
into the underworld, ethereal faeries,
Tír na nóg.
Love took me to the last foot,
leaving shore,
my love deeper than that first step
into the depth,
the ocean, another land,
sweeping me off my feet, floating
to music,
your smile,
my death.

A Diagnosis / My daughter speaks

I remember when my mother forgot simple
things, like where she left the hairbrush.

I helped her find it.
Older than my mother when she

forgot, I don't remember little things.
Impatiently, my daughter tells me I need

to see a doctor, I may even have Alzheimer's.
'I'm worried,' she says, 'you've got

the wrong names for things
and everything is lost in our house.'

She asks about breast checks, -
her friend's mum had found a lump.

That mole on my skin needs to go,
she heard about melanoma. Yet again she

asks 'What age can you get Parkinsons?'
After a half hour in the kitchen,

'Can I get a lift to my friend's house?
We're having a sleepover.'

Nesting

My garden in winter sleep
is without birds.

A neighbour's cat has scared
their search for berries, seeds,

that earthy diet of worms.
I wait for a morning song.

Except that is, those who
slip kipping's

through the chimney cowl.
They build nests through

obstacles, drop twigs, one
by one. '*For God's sake,*' I say,

'*your home is halfway
down a fluepipe.*'

I listen to the twitch
and crackle, as the sticks

smoke out my kitchen.
The stealth of it, despite

best efforts to keep them
out. Already smoked out once,

I'm reluctant to sacrifice my heat.
Even so, I can't destroy,

either bird nor nest
for the sake of my hearth.

Our Sleeping Women

I think of my grandmothers,
their faces etched in mine,
their strength sleeps in my bones.
We meet in fields of crows,
their voices speak through wind.

Old graves sloped down
from our farm. As a child,
I played house, tea sets
on tombs, innocent,
listening to spirits.
Daughters left to work
with duty not to themselves,
but others who cared little
for the objects they'd become.

From the clay they cry
the song of the crone,
dreams of the life unlived, hope
moves in the soil beneath
my feet, rises in my breath,
they call – willing me on
with their work.

Don't listen to scavengers
who have taken your use,
their fear ripping your pleasure.
Scream yourself into your body.
Starve if you need, until you're heard.

Your face ours,
your womb creator, the only real home
your self.

Fall on Me

I stood on the footpath, watched you load the car,
the radio in the background, Andrea Bocelli,
singing a duet with his son, "Fall on me." I listened,
feet clinched, tried to hold on, a last look before
you left, make it eternal, moment without words
where joy, sorrow, pride

spiral as one. I followed the curves of your curls,
faint now, arc your cheek bones, slender and strong,
never quite sure if your eyes are hazel or brown, your
innocent mischievous smile.
"What are you staring at?," you asked,
as I tried to grasp the image a photo can't take,

I wanted to say, "please don't die," and, "what if
anything happens, who will you have?"
thoughts pushed to another time, I replied,
"take care of yourself,
and try to keep out of others people's shit."
"I will be thinking about you, Mum,"

you said, shoulders above me, your arms
stretching to hug. I leaned into the boy once
cradled in my arms, two years old when sister
was born. His hands on my knees, watched her
breastfeed, repeating, as he looked in my eyes,
'I darling a mama.'

Now, four black bags, and memories my comfort,
I braved goodbye, swallowed the pea in my throat,
heart pumped in panic, said,

"You know where I am if you need me,"
"Yes mum I do, six thousand miles away!"

You reminded me to drain the lawnmower, petrol is bad
for engines, make sure to order oil for the winter.
Over our heads swallows prepared for flight,
I cried, laughed, "I'll be fine,"
as I let go of the boy
who sat on his bed, staring out to the stars, telling stories,

"there are black holes out there Mum, and when you
go through them, there are other beautiful worlds."

The Tuam Mother and Baby Home

1.

We called it The Grove,
where nature offered refuge.

I look at the photograph,
once cherished: such innocence.
This nun tended me for ten days
when my mother was ill.

Does her smile appear hard? Conceal doom?
The vow of silence has left us mute,
all questions. Did she coerce? Tyrannize?
Or was her love overwhelmed by the poverty
and overcrowding?
So many daughters dumped in fear.

What I want to know is whether these hands
that once held me have blood on them.
I see a gimp of starched linen
beneath coif, cornet, and veil,
that rigid bib. I think of the vows,
the blessings of Bons Secours.

After school, I nursed in that wing
where I and these babies were born.
Girls, there's a shadow in this place,
I'd say, We have to let the light in!
each time the walls enclosed us.

The eerie feeling haunts.
I imagine dark rooms,
darker silence.

2.

But then this lover of history,
Catherine Corless, uncovers
rumoured babies.
She persists –
reveals tiny bones, skeletal bundles
and scattered remains, young children
babies, in a septic tank.

Looking back, I shared a nursery
with these babies, their shamed mothers
segregated from the like of me.
What if, and if, my infant imaginary friends,
in babbling conversations, ghosting
themselves into my life, were thrown
into septic reservoirs and sewers?

I look again at the picture.
Neither trust nor love is possible.
The arms that held children in God's name,
are soiled.

Once more I glance again,
this time behind the nun's habit,
to a dark door, obscure shadows on the walls.
The baby she holds seems to look away,
gazing out to the world,
her eyes facing the light.

Waiting

I listen, wait,
barren, how
winter
moves across
bogs,
quiet as sky.
You
ask me
 – why?

The sun,
climbs
up behind
mountains,
movement
grows in your body,
pale tones begin
to flush.

You look
to the world,
at a willow growing
towards light.
Knowledge
buried in your bones,
tears
hint of rain - fall

as they must -
Your tears, a Saturn

moment, comfort.
There are rivers
of tears behind
every eye,
waiting to heal.
Strength,

the salt of a thousand
drops, waiting to fall.

If I Tell the Truth

I wasn't always honest
It was all about perspective,
the silent space of muted tongue
a 'yes' to presumption
how one sees Rapunzel,
protected, or snared?

I was like an old worn shoe, how
it curves into the shape of feet,
I into your desperation.
I'd watched my father, learned
his skill: natural rock, piled in layers,
roughened slab, each piece unique,
each answering to the master's eye,
making stone walls a craft.

I didn't crochet like my mother, but knew
how to catch your hook, thread deceptions
into lace, stitch, mend, plait fabrications,
seam my shawl.

Birds who fly must return to earth,
in the garden, a wood pigeon,
industrious, makes her nest.
Tolerance knows,
we all evolve, from some one family,
and you were part of mine.

Perhaps

it's all about finding
a taker for what you're offering.
I have a dark side, for instance,
my smile hides shadows,
the underside of tiny petals,
forget-me-nots, its snippet
of sky, a dark undercover.
Fibonacci sequences weave
like industrious ants
who create for the sake of it.

About the Author

 Attracta Fahy grew up on a farm in the west of Ireland, in the parish of Killererin, Co. Galway. Having a close affinity with her surroundings, she is inspired by how contemplation of nature reflects and resonates in humanity. The focus of her poetry is to explore, understand, and reveal these connections, often through the use of myth, so we can navigate our emotions, feelings, and intuition into a more integrated, and reflective way of being.

Attracta Fahy's earliest background was in Nursing and Social Care and she currently works as a Psychotherapist, Supervisor and Trainer, living in Co. Galway. Attracta is a mother of three children. She completed her MA in Writing at NUIG in 2017.

She was the October winner in Irish Times; New Irish Writing 2019, was nominated for Pushcart 2018, Best of the Web 2019, shortlisted for 2018 Over The Edge New Writer of The Year, and long listed in 2019, shortlisted for Allingham Poetry Prize 2019.

Her poems have been published in Banshee, Poetry Ireland Review, Live Encounters, A New Ulster, Boyne Berries, Bangor Literary Journal, Poethead, The Curlew, Orbis, Impspired, North West Words, Honest Ulsterman, The Lake, The Blue Nib, Cormorant, Crossways, Three Drops from a Cauldron, Fly on the Wall, Cold Coffee Stand, Enthralled, Elixir, Burning House Press and in many magazines at home and abroad. She has been included in The Blue Nib, Impspired, Her Other Language and Avalanche Anthologies.

About Fly on the Wall Press

A publisher with a conscience.
Publishing high quality anthologies on pressing issues,
chapbooks and poetry products, from exceptional poets
around the globe.Founded in 2018 by founding editor, Isabelle
Kenyon.

Other publications:
Please Hear What I'm Not Saying
(February 2018. Anthology, profits to Mind.)
Persona Non Grata
(October 2018. Anthology, profits to Shelter and Crisis Aid
UK.)
Bad Mommy / Stay Mommy by Elisabeth Horan
(May 2019. Chapbook.)
The Woman With An Owl Tattoo by Anne Walsh Donnelly
(May 2019. Chapbook.)
the sea refuses no river by Bethany Rivers
(June 2019. Chapbook.)
White Light White Peak by Simon Corble
(July 2019. Artist's Book.)
Second Life by Karl Tearney
(July 2019. Full collection)
The Dogs of Humanity by Colin Dardis
(August 2019. Chapbook.)
Small Press Publishing: The Dos and Don'ts by Isabelle Kenyon
(January 2020. Non-Fiction.)
Alcoholic Betty by Elisabeth Horan
(February 2020. Chapbook.)
Awakening by Sam Love
(March 2020. Chapbook.)

Social Media:
@fly_press (Twitter)
@flyonthewall_poetry (Instagram)
@flyonthewallpoetry (Facebook)
www.flyonthewallpoetry.co.uk

Extract from… **Planet in Peril
(Fly on the Wall Anthology)**

Available from www.flyonthewallpoetry.co.uk in
Hardback and Paperback formats.
20% of book sales go to WWF and The Climate
Coalition.

Extract from 'where she once danced' by Anne Casey

*she is drowning in a sea awash with cobalt
deadly metals fill the channels where she breathes*

*her lovely limbs are shackled down with plastics
her lungs are laced with deadly manganese
a crown of thorns to pierce her pretty head
a bed of sludge to lull her in her dreams*